Unhomely Montage-Machines

Teufel INK

BookLeaf Publishing

Presentation by *BookLeaf Publishing*

Web: www.bookleafpub.com

E-mail: info@bookleafpub.com

ISBN: 9789357440752

First edition 2023

For Andy, Jack, and Jasmine.

PREFACE

"We protect our minds by an elaborate system of abstractions, ambiguities, metaphors and similes from the reality we do not wish to know too clearly; we lie to ourselves, in order that we may still have the excuse of ignorance, the alibi of stupidity and incomprehension."
Aldous Huxley

Can Truth be arrived at through the imposition of patterns, rules, and methods? Indeed, is there a Truth to be unveiled within the universe? A curtain to be raised, by Dorothy and her deficient company, to unveil the mechanics of reality? This a poor analogy, given Truth, in that film at least, is seen ultimately to be the by-product of the machinations of those who know reality is malleable and work it for their selfish ends. Should Truth even be capitalised? Romanticised? Idealised? Singularised? Or is it many truths that shoot up momentarily in a purely relational and subjective union of prejudice and opportunity? Is truth both accidental and occidental? Did I only ask if truth was "accidental and occidental" because those two words rhyme and offer some sense of radicalistic, revolutionary aspect to what would otherwise be a very beige, middle-class aesthetic? I quote myself more often than I should.

This, far from exhaustive list of conundrums and ponderings, are some of the questions this collection of poetry does not even begin to answer. This is a work of masturbatory mysticism, idiocy, and structure-less perplexity. I am confused, why shouldn't you be too?

Over 21 days, I endeavoured to write 21 poems. Ostensibly giving myself some guiding principle, some method, and structure, each day I drew and reflected upon a Tarot card from the traditional Marseilles deck. Focussing on the images on the cards, I wrote out of the images, symbols and titles, often finding myself in unforeseen territories. Formatively, the idea was to give a structural and thematic aid from which to work, yet as the writing continued, I realised that the language that was being generated between myself and the images became less and less anchored in the chosen card; instead the concepts and words became ripped and exposed, a cacophony of syllables that, in truth, belies both the excitement and fear I feel in the face of an infinitely fascinating and infuriating universe.

I am fascinated with the structures and the categories we use every day. I am fascinated by how we develop these structures and categories to help diffuse our understandable terror. Rather than seeing and accepting the vast empty space interrupted by the distant-dim light of a billion blinding stars; you saw a man hunting, and called him a god.

I tried to write how I am; confused and enthralled and bursting with feeling everything all at once, all the time. Perhaps this is schizopoetics.

Some lyrical; some unnecessarily long; some short and brutal; varying rhyme schemes; a melting-pot of measure and meter; some based on Lacanian psychology; some on the aristocratic philosophy of Deleuze and Guattari; some based on what I couldn't stop obsessing about; some cobbled together, sorry, montaged from previous writing that somehow interrupted my focus and took me to places I'd rather not have visited again; some urgent; some necessary. But, was there a truth, which rose? A beacon of light? Verisimilitudes? Bollocks was there; just the unheard, unread ramblings of a drowning man.

I am a lie, beguiled by rhythm and ruled by rhyme.

I DREW THE SUN

(Active masculine side. Rational intelligence, energy, vitality, loyalty, courage, and generosity; expression of firmness and stability. Joy, clarity, love, friendship, dazzlement.)

And yet we still dance,
Looking forward, looking down,
To enjoy, to bask, to feel the grass that
Grows because of what you give.
Wreathed in flowers, flares brief, blissful
falsities powerful.
I only see because of the light you give
Allows. A brick wall behind me,
A certain security of what this was,
What this was and what could
Stop being;
Foetal, ancient, and forgetful,
My collective memory stumbles, imperious,
crippled.
A duet that has slept and danced with Psyche
and Apollo.
They have, respectfully, assured us
That they will never leave us
Until we, bandy-legged with unbridled joy reach
a point of complete quantum dispersion.

(On reaching said coordinates, it is politely, yet firmly requested that we all, hand-in-hand, return to
That singular point from which you know you could not have helped but depart).

Those rays that hold all colour, all life, all that is life, all gold
Now obscured by frosted windows held by all that is limp and old,
All that lies through a history of truths untold.
Shine now, do not drip upon pallid skin,
Mine that craves the warmth promised,
Not delivered, stolen.
Solar trickledown economics that should otherwise be pregnant with excess.
I squint.
She squats.
I stare at the sun, like we all have done, and see the lustre of gold melt into the flesh-red impoverished eyelids.
We burn white before welcoming eternal night.
The sun.
Your treasures.
My piss.
They are all toys, the colour of sulphur.

I DREW THE MAGICIAN

(Represents the beginning and the capacity to grow, dominating the elements. A person in action, lively, gifted in abilities, creativity, charm, and cunning. Youth, security, astuteness.)

I could not stand upon Hasting's shore
Feel the wind blow so deeply, resolutely,
With all the power of your hateful gales.
I could not withstand, as I stood upon that West Hill
In my charming neighbourhood,
The oncoming storm of perpetual prejudice.

Be quiet you winds, stand firm you earth,
Be still the fire that boils water already disturbed.
Be still, hold firm, be Heart be Soul;
Be fervent in ideal and let love for all not stir.
Let me not forget, that I pulled Death and put him back.
Let me not forget I then drew the Fool
And turned him back. Why was that?
Because we are Magicians,
We have power over the Pack.

I DREW THE CHARIOT

(Capacity to choose which direction to take. An adventure, the courage of those who know what they want, flaunting. Success, travel, control, determination, triumph.)

Crown'd and scepter'd I stand, holding no reigns
For the Beasts that tear me apart,
Under a ruling canopy of stars.
A spectre, a burden.

Crown'd and scepter'd, I fall beset and besieged
By the unbearable weight
Of impossible, endless choice.

For four eternal days
I have again been locked in
By my endlessly open doors.
It is within this space, made liminal
By the forces of nostalgia and unease,
That I wait to see what I myself will make of me,
And watch the hours, the days, the years
Slip serrated through possibilities.

For myself and in myself; gnossienne.

A little house, underground, all the trappings of a home
But cold, dark, weird.
Here is the main road, Here, the way out;
A garden, a water park, a kitchenette, and car storage.
This little house of Becomings exacerbates sensuality,
All things occurring at once;
Nerves flooded by pleasure and pain forever
Oscillating in Lacanian jouissance.
My eyes are inverted and my stomach sits like a sphere
Rotating upon a pin-point totem pole, rising higher
Until it unfolds itself like a flower bud.
Like a flower bud, I cascade back upon me,
Cradling my body with anther;
Lifting me up, pulling me back into ovaries,
In which I gestate, grow again and again,
Repeat the process.

I DREW THE BELOVED

(Capacity to choose; a fork in the road where the one of two options must be decided. Feelings, love, a love triangle. Choice, trust, falling in love, indecision, balance.)

Lands once broken, now will rise up against
Those chosen by themselves to pin us down.
Come earth, come dirt, and bury that false crown
That steals from her people with tricks and
feints.
And is it us that dances in bright paints?
And is it us to build this paper town
Upon our beloved England's wise ground?
Blessed heads of tissue Saints do disappoint.
No ground will be out of bounds to fresh minds
Eager to renew that which we had lost.
No breath further to be taken from us
If taken from us to enslave mankind.
Don't build Jerusalem at any cost,
Earth, once pure; for wealth and war used; now
cursed.

I DREW THE HIEROPHANT

(Capacity to go beyond the material aspect of things. Authority that resides in spiritual power; a figure capable of being an intermediary between two worlds. Spirituality, vocation, guidance, wisdom, mediation.)

I would rather than Hierophant be,
An Acephale living for and in ecstasy;
To escape rather than abuse thought to
Develop a relationship with the One
Or Many believed to have created us.
I renounce the state, the grey suits
Of formality and vice, and so too
I renounce the Church and their indentured, diminished mice,
I renounce all and everything that will try to reduce the universe
and all myriad life to an extension of itself.

Follow still, and dance with the Headless; agitating the void.
Shake shackles of function and set fire to reason.
For, in that system that

Tears us apart for servitude to capital lies the truth of long-buried Theseus;
That Labyrinth, the Minotaur, and the favoured son are one -
A hermetically sealed prison cell that secures none.

I DREW THE HANGED MAN

(A moment of stagnation, when nothing is getting done. Propensity to sacrifice, a change of perspective. Deprivation, spiritual elevation, victimism, initiation, betrayal.)

Suspended in this moment -
A moment drawn complete
By Mnemosyne and Aion,
When they finally never meet.
A moment reversed, perpetual, constant, and indefatigable
Like the Ouroboros, the eternal prey preyed upon eternally by itself;
The snake rejuvenescing, bathing in tempests of time;
Like the abysmal image of the depths made topless,
Like the Möbius strip and bottles of Klein:
I am lost in two dimensions yet I feel fine.

My heart is above my mouth, and it pours out.
I shout, only to find my toes tremble.
If I could ask to be reassembled, reconstituted, and reformed

To start my day again, I would not,
I am content upside down.

And was it you who drew these ropes about my feet?
You who sculpted me into this Borromean knot
With one tree with life replete
The other's life excreted?
Was it you who hitched me to this branch, demanding complicity?
Who said, disbelievingly, suspend disbelief?

The veil slips from my eyes finally
Due to invariable forces intent on trapping me
And in so doing, set me completely free.

I am, as I hang, neither on the ground nor with Celestials,
A transcendental axiom in and of myself:
Entirely self-sufficient,
A terror to myself,
Yet rigorously immanent alongside the real
As I am ejected ex uterine into the engine of perpetual invention.

So here I swing, a thing with mechanics exposed,
Augmented, unforeseen, and full of possibilities,
Ungoverned and structureless,

When immanence and transcendence,
Hybridised, dyadic,
Consumed and consummated,
My senses slithered in perpetual displacement.

I have, as I hang, no point of departure or arrival
No death drive nor sense of survival.
No singular god-head as an object of meditation,
Just a sublime, continuous recapitulation.
I am an Abbey of Crime
I am a library of unwritten pages, in which both
monk and beast have fucked throughout the
ages.

I have, as I hang, confounded space
I have, as I hang, confounded time,
Non-materialisation, non-territorialisation.
Simply through methodologies of forgetfulness
and idiocy.
I am, as I hang, not distinct from my other
My interior is synonymous with your exterior,
though approached in mirror form.
I have, as I hang, neither lived nor died
Seen nor unseen
Please never let me be untied.

I DREW THE HIGH PRIESTESS

(The power of knowledge and receptive feminine knowledge. A phase during which importance is given to reflection, to accumulating knowledge. Wisdom, intuition, reserve, mystery.)

And what still day is born,
Through the Sapphic union of the crescent silver moon
And precious spectrumed dawn?
What balance cradled, what calm held
Over violent seas, untouched by the faintest breeze?
These waters unsullied by Romantic's lusty oars
That leaves no shore unkissed nor forlorn,
But pregnant, if pregnant be:
A moment rebirthed in eternity,
A reflection not retreating,
Nor staking false claim
To lands founded in blood and held for profit or fame.

I DREW THE STAR

(Hope. Following one's vocation, living in harmony. Situation in which one feels at peace and in synch with their own nature. Beauty, far-sightedness, desires, following one's own path.)

Please guide me through this…

We can't be with you right now
But, I could really do with a little…

Your call is very important to us
I need to say something poignant, I have only a few…

You are 13th in the queue
Thalia, please pick up, there is a forest I would love to summon up in imagery

Press 5 for customer service
Erato, then, please how do I write a swollen heartbroken?

Press 4 for technical issues
Polyhymnia, then, if this poem is of stars,
please….

If you would like to speak to a member of our
team, say "yes"
Yes

I'm sorry, I did not hear that, if you would like
to…
Yes. Yes!
All of our operatives are otherwise
engaged, please hold.
FFS.

I DREW JUDGEMENT

(Rebirth, a calling, reawakening. A new phase of life, definitive and irreversible renewal. Capacity to be ready to change. Calling, manifestation, repentance.)

A fire, in devastating waves,
Ripped through Old Town last night.
Decrepit timbers, long-seeking renewal, razed
Slipping through midnight ash.
And you all stood around,
Ogling the destruction like it was the 90s and you
You were on your tea break with Page 3
Sipping another milky cup of tea as this scepter'd isle
Took another slump in its economy.

"And why the inferno now?" Rose the jeers
"When, like a knock-kneed beggar, unmoving
This building has remained for years
Sealed off with scaffolding
On the edge of under cliff avenue."
No impetus to change, in Britain now,
Unless for reasons of lost revenue

“No need”, they said, as homes and hearth were bled,
“To feed a sickly cow
Before bolting it through its head.”

I DREW JUSTICE

(The need to find balance, equity, and impartiality. Capacity to make judgements, situation, the right person or decision. Equilibrium, harmony, law, logic, impassibility.)

When your house is stricken,
Your last card played,
Think of God and how
Despite this, He is neither moved
Nor seeks to move.

Come rain, come storm,
Come across young lives stolen and torn,
Think of Him and take warmth;
Nothing that you suffer through
Will touch your Lord - Impassible as He is.
Impassibility is an archaic idea,
Which, as I read, seems to mean a complete lack of empathy…
So, here's His Church, here's His steeple;
Unfeeling stone, cold steel, unheard people.
I will brook no sociopathic celestial being
To govern a universe,
In which the primacy of pleasure and pain undoubtedly reigns.

No god for me, who does not feel
The love, the hate, and all between,
Felt so keenly through a life in which He
demands we serve.

I DREW THE UNNAMED CARD

(Death and rebirth; change and transformation. Invitation to manifest one's own essence, without superstructures, paying attention only to the essential. Cut, end, loss.)

Seems strange to reduce to the singular,
A battle invariably lost against entropy.
It is the insta-story ego versus the second law of thermodynamics.
It is Jesus holding back ΔS.
Mohammed sweeping dirt under the rug.
Buddha frantically cleaning the crime scene
Before we notice that, exsanguine the body lies.
I drink to a plethora of gods
The possibility of an endlessly variable anima,
To forgetting who I was before I become something other,
Over again and over again.
To the big toe clenching in the dirt.
To my pineal eye bursting.
To my stomach, which is swollen,
Containing a vast maze of libraries written in languages
Of which my tongue cannot still yet conceive.

So no, not one.
Many.

Cry disorder and dispersion
Set out screaming, breaking the firmament open with joy and laughter.
My joy, my laughter, a knife through the heart of the scion,
Who has, with his scythe-like heirlooms,
Gathered our myriad wealth and gathered for only himself.
So no, not one,
Many.
So no, not one,
Many.

I DREW THE FOOL THEN I DREW THE HERMIT

(The Fool is the only Arcanum without a number. The man who continues along his path of evolution leaves reason behind to allow his creative energy to express itself. Joy, enthusiasm, freedom, madness, innocence ----- ------ The Hermit: wisdom, research, relationship with time, old age. A period when there is a need to look inward and spend some time alone. Prudence, silence meditation, hermitage, widowhood.)

Joy – Prudence

The landscape seems to extend infinitely...
The sky too...
Vast and indecipherable,
Into the space pour tears
– Space tears and ruptures –
As we reintroduce ourselves.
The movement of the air that flew undisturbed
Is excited and jostled by our presence;
It slows and sweeps around,
Investigating the new agent.
Weep for the lost horizon.

A Fool on a journey to meet a Hermit,
Who cautions against frolicking.

Enthusiasm – silence

And still, these images taunt me
With their wilderness and confident loneliness.
Their peaks and valleys rise and fall like
economic graphs:
All meet the smooth eternal stretch
Of deep blue and sky blue,
Striated space and striated finances
That will be when we return,
Not as they used to be.
Towards equality and unity, we march,
In our solitary cells.
A Hermit waits for a Fool;
Begins to rupture the silence in enthusiasm.

Freedom – Hermitage

I have data fatigue.
Statistics, graphs, and charts have disassociated
me.
I check the figures daily and see
The abstracted numbers of 933
More dead:
933
More intricately connected lives,

Interweaved with exponentially more other lives
Who in turn…..who in turn:
Where n equals someone you do not know
multiplied by y
(Someone who is left behind).
"I am free," says the Fool, bound for the
Hermitage.

Madness – Meditation.

I think better when I am travelling;
For the moment no movement.
I will take your figures and cartographise you;
Each incremental increase moves me
Across the earth to a different location,
Both real and imagined –
The digital realisation of mathematical
abstraction.
I find myself in the deserts of In Amguel.
I find myself in the Kara Sea, in Xudun,
In the Gulf of Guinea, Seychelles, Tchirozerine,
And the Norwegian Sea.
Cadaveric cartographies move me closer to your
realities.
We are still connected – I travel so that you are
remembered.
The Hermit has sat silent, meditating,
Awaiting the madness of his friend, the Fool.

Innocence – Widowhood

Rock formations spring up like couch grass.
Franny recounts a dream: “There is a desert”.
She said.
Smooth space meets a vast geological rupture,
These cliffs leak into the sea.
These vast, vast walls meet the cold, cold waters
And these cold, cold waters meet the blue, blue sky
– A striation of space made beautiful through its leakages.
Writing itself unfolds like a camel ride,
With unpredictable speeds, slownesses, spurts, and stoppages.
A gulf.
Not a void.
Instead a space in which,
Two forces embrace and unify.
This is not an abyss,
Nor is it a difference that separates and classifies;
It is a plateau on which the velocity of a vast body of water
Caresses and communicates with the land
Which in turn has its own paths moulded
And altered accordingly.
A multitude of islands,
A conglomerate of platforms

Interconnected out-croppings.
Strata meet strata meet strata
Then they fall away only to rise again.
We are archipelagos in ourselves:
Not continuous lands,
We are ever inconsistent but consistently rise in
Surprising architectures of being.
The spaces between these architectures are
The true frames of fascination.
The Fool had not realised, the Hermit had lost
his wife.

I DREW THE GOD HOUSE

(Change, revelation. Breaking free of something that was keeping you prisoner; possibility to manifest oneself. Sudden events. Creative energy, lack of control, collapse, fear.)

The plans drawn up, permission granted
A tower was built, but slightly slanted,
Torn down again, and again restarted
Whilst families evicted and brokenhearted
Sat asking, for shelter and safety
From the men paid repeatedly for basic
necessities.

These towers will be built for all of us
So said the slogan on the side of the bus
So do be patient, do wait in turn
To live in towers built to burn.

I DREW TEMPERANCE

(Balance, gentility, attention. Patience, perseverance and measurement; capacity to combine different energies when moving forward, moderating instincts. Harmony, stagnation.)

We sat down, like many times before,
Round the kitchen table, food eaten, wine poured.
We set about breaking the week apart;
How did it end? Usually worse than the start.
She slipped through her thoughts, sporadically
Falling across an infinity of "oh, and anotherthings..."
I thought I sat there quite patiently, until
I felt my leg jigging up and down tremulously;
Keep focussed, I said to me, and try to not interrupt...
But, I want to reply before I have forgot.
"Don't be abrupt....
Let me just finish...
God I can't get a word in edgeways"
She says after I uttered, one syllable dazed and lonely.
"Well, fine, then, go on, if you must."

It’s just, I’ve been trying to write more and would love to share
My thoughts with you, as no one else will care.
I’ll speak them out if that helps? You don’t have to read.
“Okay, then, but do hurry”
I read them out; words that had been bled from me;
On beauty, on pain, on random philosophy,
On everything that came to mind first
Caught in meter, wrapped in verse.
“You don’t put any emotion into speaking, it’s dull, your voice.”
And, with no choice, the words grabbed from my mouth
“Here’s how you do it”
She began to read so eloquently
Just like you’re supposed to do with poetry.
“See? That’s how you do it,
Now, back to me.”
I hope one day you’ll hear me again
Know the words of love and fire and soul within
But how would you, Em?
You’ll never bloody read them.
But, on the off chance that you do,
Just as a post-script, a note
To the one on whom I do truly dote,
Know that poetry often deals with imagined insecurities,

Broad brushstrokes, subjective realities, see?
Paints a life rife in ironies, believe me?
Because she never really said what I wrote
And I suppose it's best not to write,
When I've been sleeping on the sofa for three
cold nights,
My spine bent into a question mark,
Like the questions, I wish she'd ask me
About all my endless thoughts and endless
Endless, endless fucking poetry.

I DREW THE EMPEROR

(Self-confidence and material security. A phase of tranquillity, a mature figure, a role of power, self-reliance. Stability, authority, concreteness, decision, power.)

There's a bric-a-brac shop on St Leonard's
seafront,
Sells odds and ends, furniture, lamps,
And
Hand-
Me-
Downs.
Flamboyantly calls itself "20th Century Art and
Design",
But it's just stuff no one really wants.
Three floors deep, chthonic,
Past art deco-mirrors sloganned
With dated images of buxom wenches
Having pints of Guinesses,
"Just the tonic!"
Or would-be, should-be, toothless kids
Smiling with bottles of coke unlidded
Past rows of moth-eaten military jackets,
Cracked vases and ashtrays
Sullied opaque with sentimental touch

And hacking coughs.
In the depths, past it all,
Upon the cracked paint of an unlit wall
Framed, famed, and most imperious;
There's Vladimir Ilyich Uyanov,
Statesmanlike portrayed,
Looking out over his new land
And waiting for that red wave,
To wash upon his new shores,
Shores peopled with unwanted memorabilia.
His power forgotten, his image orphaned,
But his words, resonating with us,
The bargain-hunters, the canIhaveabitoff's and
the whatsthebestyoucando's
Cos it's just like Lenin said:
"I am the Walrus."

I DREW THE EMPRESS

(Ideas that become fertile and create; an action already underway and ready to bear fruit.
Capacity to love; fertility, a true pregnancy.
Practicality, decision, power and intelligence.)

It was after all this…
Albion, throned and moneyed.

It was during this…
3.9 million children below the poverty line.

It was after all this…
You broke our families.

Perfidious Albion
You have broken trust.
Perfidious Albion
You have left us lost.
Perfidious Albion
Leaders never voted.
Perfidious Albion,
Liars in luxury.
Lives hard-fought for, lie in tatters under your golden-heeled boots.

I DREW THE MOON

(Feminine receptive side. Intuitions, dreams, sensitivity, emotions, memories, receptiveness, instinctive part, hidden things. Mystery, ambiguity, passivity.)

I saw the truth, stepping from my door
Reflected in the sea, I swore
I saw the truth, a lobster aggressing the shore.
Two dogs, lost, howling at you, as they caught
coloured petals in their jaws.
And you, the truth, shining up from the water;
Through changing each day, from pregnant
sphere to sabre-curve,
Remained, constantly changed.
And in me too, reflected from some sacred depth
A changing voice, consistent, still swarmed on
my breath
Fluctuating and nomadic – a life of glorious
inconsistency.
And what do I feel this is?
Dared.
Dreaded.
De
bil
i

tate
d
.
And I guess that I am here.
Could you not jump, if you wouldn't mind?
Could you?
Stop filming.
Stop filming.
Across the waterway, barely demarcated by
Google maps.
Smash him in the face.
You did it.
Shout. Walk up a hill. Feel justified.

And that carriage is late again.
            5 minutes – just in time
So I taught you 3 years ago, I thought you would
think….?
            It is as it has been thought to have
been, but they said they did it for you.
Shuffle. Shuffle. Nothing moves. Joy of a child.
Stopped. Not comforted – your own. Bang.
Zoom
Shuffle. Shuffle.
ZOOM. Bang.
Don't you fucking know who I fucking am?

I DREW THE WHEEL OF FORTUNE

(The ups and downs of life; a cycle in perpetual motion, ability to accept one's destiny: a stroke of good or bad luck. Destiny, chance, conclusion, fate.)

My heart aches and the Fool steals off with joy.
My sense, as though dulled and drowned in the sand
Is conned by Magicians, now redeployed
To steal your life, a friend wrenched from my hand.
Tis' not through envy of High Priestesses,
But being lost in Dalston again my friend,
That you, wheel-spinning, keep me down here
In some jail of Empresses'
Of locked doors and bleached hallways with no end;
An Emperor, now dethroned cries havoc.

No Hierophant will allow me access
To a mind lost in tragic accident
Lovers we were if love is art professed,
Danced, Kafka through the night, wine-kissed, well-meant

Stop that Chariot crashing through my dreams,
Full of possibilities dispossessed,
With bold Strength ripping wild beasts' jaws apart,
And shadow struck seems;
Not Hermit born, but left, nevertheless,
Yet still not faded in my scratching memory:

The Wheel of Fortune brings me back to you
What scattered writings of yours still unknown,
No Justice, armed, blind, swords swing at the few
No this way or that, signs unseen, unshone;
Where I, upside down, a Hanged Man, strung, done
Where my face grows pale, and sorrow-full dies;
Where unnumbered death sits eating your problems
And floating joy moves on,
Where Temperance cannot keep her calming eyes,
For new balance lies when stolid hearts condemn.

Away! away! I will not Devil draw
Not charioted by decision unmade

Towers are built and built to be unsure,
        A love for a people, a love in shade:
And I am taken along by the Star,
        She guides me, simultaneously One
Silvered Moon cuts through; eyes, grey clouds,
and spoons;
                        But here there is no light,
        But I still, since you've gone stared into
the Sun
            Through a life too quickly taken, a life
undone.

The Judgement I make, though not through my
feet
        Says much of those friends that fall from
now,
The World, it's ours made incomplete
        I come back to you an ally avowed.
A Nightingale, Daniel, fell far from the roof,
A Nightingale, Daniel, fell far from the crowd.

I DREW THE DEVIL

I DREW THE DEVIL

(Restrictions. Dependence on something or something. Constrictions that provoke anger. Personal magnetism. Sensuality and sexuality, total lack of self-control. Psycho-physical energy.)

Lost son, fallen, built
Banks deep in the broken hills;
Stripped fruit trees bare.

I DREW THE WORLD

(Obtaining something you desire. Perfection, harmony, wholeness among the different aspects of existence. The desired result, happy closure of a cycle, attaining one's desires.)

I drew the world today, though not a perfect circle,
Drew too, those cradled within arching arms, uncertain
As blindly they sat, both breaking and mortal,
Feeling that her rough skin drew back, uncurtained;
They touched the flesh of undulating earth
Prostrate and languorous before them.
She wept for cold scars made centuries deep,
And was seen trembling throughout still lighted night.
But did she wail for dreams harmoniously failed?
No; it was us in great pains wracked by life ungrown.
Listen, you captains of industry, hear wind-born cries
As you tear her asunder. Her belly you mined

Her lungs sullied, her heart irreparably plundered.

So now to join, at least on paper,
Two points drawn of an imperfect circle.
We have not, with loving arms gathered,
She who likewise lovingly gathers;
Our time is up, but hers is not
As all life stretches from her womb,
For we, who sought to profit; now alone entombed.

I DREW STRENGTH

(Courage that wins over brute force and over instincts; victory that can be attained with intelligence without using force. Physical and psychic energy, instinct, lucidity, control.)

I am only left with strength,
After all this,
Strength to see what comes;
Strength to wake and live
Strength to hold the hand that needs
A tender guide through
Heaven-born winds.
Nibble-nibble-gnaw-gnaw
The wind, the wind.
And so my house still stands,
Built to last as long as us, and no more,
Nothing I need needs to persist longer than that.
Strength to be fragile
To fail
And in failing, stand, not fallen.
Remembered for as long as memory comforts or intrigues.

www.ingramcontent.com/pod-product-compliance
Lightning Source LLC
Chambersburg PA
CBHW051741130826
49812CB00033B/954